Some Thoughts About Relationships

COLIN WRIGHT

Asymmetrical Press
Missoula, Montana

Published by Asymmetrical Press
Missoula, Montana.

Library of Congress Cataloging-In-Publication Data
Some Thoughts About Relationships / Colin Wright — 1st ed.
ISBN: 978-1-938793-88-2
eISBN: 978-1-938793-87-5
WC: 17,150
1. Relationships. 2. Self-Help. 3. Partnerships. 4. Personal Growth.
5. Communication.

Cover design by Colin Wright
Formatted in beautiful Montana
Printed in the U.S.A.

Publisher info:
Website: www.asymmetrical.co
Email: howdy@asymmetrical.co
Twitter: @asympress

ASYM METR ICAL

ACKNOWLEDGEMENTS

A great big thanks to the folks who helped me whip this book into suitable shape for publication:

Tim Blattmann, Liam Page, Jason Strickland, Faith Radford, Julianna Smith, Isabel Pinaud, Autumn La Duke, Simon, Fernandes, Andrew Miles, Alexandra Doligkeit, Belle Betsy Orcullo, Tonya van der Wal, Joni Edison, Santiago Rial, Tej Dhawan, Ken Willard, and Evie Socarras.

Any typos or other mistakes are probably the result of me ignoring their damn good advice.

For the wonderful people I've been fortunate to date in my lifetime. Thank you so much for the time we shared, the limits we tested, and for teaching me so very much.

The only real security is not in owning or possessing,
not in demanding or expecting, not in hoping, even.
Security in a relationship lies neither in looking back to
what it was, nor forward to what it might be,
but living in the present and accepting it as it is now.

—ANNE MORROW LINDBERGH

I don't need anyone to rectify my existence. The most profound
relationship we will ever have is the one with ourselves.

—SHIRLEY MACLAINE

Some Thoughts About Relationships

FOREWORD

By Joshua Fields Millburn

If I could go back in time and give my eighteen-year-old self one nugget of advice, it would be this: *You can't change the people around you, but you can change the people around you.*

You see, for most of my life, nearly all of my relationships—intimate or otherwise—were predicated on proximity and convenience. I made friends with coworkers in the same office building. I dated women because we grew up in the same town. I hung out with folks who were closest to me (geographically) but not closest to me (behaviorally).

While there's nothing wrong with building bonds with the people you're forced to spend time with each day (in fact, I'd encourage it), the problem is that we all have the same twenty-four hours in a day; and so, if we allocate all of our time and attention—our two most precious resources—to people who don't share our standards, then it's hard to build stable, meaningful relationships.

I know this now, of course, looking in the rearview, because, after thirty-four years of trial and error, I've finally surrounded myself with people who have values similar to my own.

I first met Colin Wright in an unconventional way: via Twitter, in 2009, the month after my marriage disintegrated. Although we were thousands of miles way—him in New Zealand, me in Dayton, Ohio—we established a friendship based on common interests.

One of the first things I noticed about Colin is that he's a good person. At first glance, though, I was certain his nice-guy demeanor was only a well-crafted facade. I mean, could someone really be this honest and open and caring? Probably not. At least not from what I'd experienced in my Midwestern propinquity bubble. However, as I've gotten to know him these past six years, I've learned that Colin's outward appearance is a genuine reflection of what is going on inside: *what he says* and *who he is* are congruent.

Now, that's not to say that he and I have the same personalities. We don't. In fact, even though we have similar values, we often arrive at those values via different beliefs, which means we'll debate specifics all day long, but, because our values are sound, we rarely disagree on the principles themselves.

For years, I've asked Colin to write a book containing his thoughts on relationships. *Some Thoughts About Relationships* is that book. The following pages are filled with principles—what Colin calls "Policies"—that can be applied to business relationships, friendships, and lovers. While many of the insights in this book might seem as if they were written with a bent toward intimate connections, I believe that every "Policy" herein is valuable no mater the context of the relationship.

It's worth mentioning that most of the topics breached in each chapter are somewhat unconventional—and that's a good thing: too often, convention forces us to "go with the flow," but then, in time, the flow eventually drags us to the falls, which we don't realize until it's too late. Colin's thoughts on relationships will help you paddle upstream, avoid the falls, and curate new, worthwhile relationships grounded in trust and caring and, most import, shared values.

CONTENTS

INTRO

I don't drink coffee after 3pm.

This is one of my many "policies," a term I use for the guidelines I've discovered work well for me, but which aren't laws chiseled into stone tablets, handed down by elders, backed by oral tradition, and broken only at my mortal soul's peril.

I sleep much better when I keep my caffeine consumption time-restricted, but I'll still sometimes break my Coffee Policy, consuming a cup at 3:30pm when I'm really on a roll and want to keep my morning momentum going just a little longer. Or maybe I'll have a post-dinner espresso while visiting a country, or family, where after-food digestives are part and parcel for a pleasant and sociable evening. While on long distance road trips which require extended, late-night drives, I'll banish my coffee restriction completely. For a time, at least.

This book is organized around policies. Much like my Coffee Policy, they are guidelines that I know will be periodically bent and broken. These ideas have become best-practices for me and what I want out of relationships, but are in no way one-size-fits-all. The policies that follow are a good starting point for developing your own guidelines, but needn't be bought into wholesale to be effective.

My earnest hope is that these concepts and perspectives will help catalyze more intentionality on the topic of relationships, spark more productive conversations and self-reflection, and maybe even provide an introduction to some unfamiliar facets of partnerships. That being said, identifying what you actually *want* in a relationship, figuring out how to make that happen in real life, and doing so in a healthy, maintainable fashion, is up to you.

A strange thing happens when your relationships become more balanced and healthy: the storylines portrayed on television, in movies, and written about in novels seldom make much sense. Not all stories, just those that revolve around distrust and deceit.

Broken or misaligned relationships are a common trope, featured in everything from romance novels to science fiction, in westerns and Shakespearean plays. Someone hurts someone else, and revenge is sought. Or someone cheats, and another character questions everything. Or someone fails as a spouse, or a would-be-spouse, by failing to "know" their partner on a deep level, without words needing to be spoken. Heartbreak, confusion, or murder ensues.

I understand why these stories are told the way they are told. I'm not blind to the appeal of drama and intrigue. But I do feel I'm being forced to suspend disbelief pretty much all the time. There's no way we're *that* bad at communicating with each other, *that* bad at making our needs known, *that* bad at managing our relationships and keeping them balanced, *that* bad at setting expectations and living up to them. Are we?

We are. Sometimes, anyway. I don't know if it's life imitating art or the other way around. Likely it's a bit of both. The dramatized conflict is informed by what actually happens between partners, and people living in the real world are informed by what they see on screens, read in fiction, and watch on stages. This is how relationships *are*, we're told. They're difficult and emotion-driven, and you may have to fight and strain to make them work.

This book is an attempt to unspool some of the ideas we're fed about relationships so that we might give them a closer look. So that we might consider why they are the way they are before going back out into the world, hopefully with a new perspective on the matter. Perhaps we'll glean some ideas about how relationships could be better approached and maintained, and maybe even achieve clarity as to why we do what we do when we're building and navigating the connections we share with the most important people in our lives.

Relationships have the potential to drastically improve our lives, or to sucker punch us in the emotional gut. Impactful as these interpersonal ties can be, it's worth the effort to become more familiar with them, question a lot of our default notions that surround them, and calibrate them to best suit our needs and those of the people we care about.

This is a book for people who want it all when it comes to relationships: something tailor-made for their unique beliefs, goals, desires, and lifestyles. This is a book for people who aren't afraid to ask, "How might we do this better?"

RATIONALITY POLICY

The Rationality Policy is simple, but is also probably the most important concept in this book.

Being rational in relationships means that you acknowledge cause and effect, the possibility of iterative improvement, and the potential to pull apart and assess problems to find solutions.

Being irrational means that you rely on a storyline to make things right: that if you just believe hard enough, want it bad enough, or go through enough struggle, life will work itself out. No assessment possible, no change necessary.

Declaring relationships or love to be beyond human understanding is irrational: it means you've given up on trying to have any control, and have instead decided to leave the failure or success of your partnership to chance. It's essentially saying, "Hopefully someone else will make this work for us, because I'm not willing to put in the effort." We can do better than that.

Relationships needn't be irrational to be valuable, romantic, and fulfilling. The idea that they need be, that one must be crazy-in-love, head-over-heels, not thinking and just leaping, is a harmful concept, and is part of why there are so many volatile, fragile couplings in the world.

Opting for irrationality in your relationships keeps valuable discussions and potential solutions to problems forever out of reach. It limits your potential for growth, because there's no foundation upon which to grow: it's out of your hands.

A rational basis for how you deal with your partner, on the other hand, means you can safely throw yourself into things without apprehension. If something goes wrong, you'll assess the issue and figure out a solution that works for everyone involved. Rather than spending all of your time hoping and wishing, you can make course adjustments as necessary, and more fully enjoy the time you spend with your partner.

Remember this policy, as it's the basis for any practical contemplation of relationships. Without rationality, relationships often become little more than sources of angst, pain, and confusion. A rational mindset helps us remember that relationships should be considered and intentional, not dependent on luck.

COMMUNICATION POLICY

If rationality is the foundation of a successful relationship, communication is the mortar that holds together whatever structure you decide to build.

Communication is vital and shockingly underutilized. It's the linchpin that holds a relationship together, and yet most of us ignore it in favor of hollow, trick-based solutions to our partnership problems. We imbibe supermarket magazine list-fulls of questionable advice in the off-chance we might remedy our sickly connections. We bow down to well-meaning-but-ultimately-flawed theories that have been passed down from one confused, uncertain generation to the next.

The Communication Policy contains three main points of consideration.

The first is to remember that everyone speaks a different language, and not just in the English, Spanish, Japanese sense of the word. The vocabularies we use for things are different from person to person, and as such, incredibly important words like "relationship" and "love" and even "communication" will mean something slightly, or vastly, different to each individual who uses them.

For example, to me, "love" might be a word I throw around

casually, doling it out to acquaintances, a movie I particularly liked, or a cupcake I just ate. To someone else, the word "love" may be reserved for only the most intimate and important connections in one's life, like family and significant others. For you, the word "love" may be held back until a particular point in a relationship, or only during special moments with family.

Similarly, you may use the word "relationship" when casually dating, while others will keep it in reserve until there's a more formal commitment. "Communication" to me may indicate a particular brand of deep, explorative conversation, while to you, it can also apply to emoji-heavy text messages sent throughout the day, a hug held a second longer than necessary, or other types of casual, even non-verbal means of expression.

There's a spectrum of meaning for all words, and figuring out their specific significance for each of us, beyond the dictionary definition, is how we turn what might otherwise be a garbled connection into a crystal clear channel of information exchange. Sussing out the specifics allows us to converse so that both speaker and listener understand what's going on in the other person's mind more directly, rather than being forced to translate what they're hearing into what's *actually* meant; a process that can often result in mistranslations and misunderstandings.

Second, it's important to communicate goals and expectations. This may seem like a no-brainer, but it's an easy step to skip, often without even realizing it.

Consider that at the beginning of relationships we tend to tip-toe around certain issues, not wanting to rock the boat, and hoping to see where things might go before we commit to any hardline stances.

This means that when someone we're dating indicates that they're looking forward to having kids and starting a family, you might let it slide for the moment and see how the relationship progresses before telling them you don't want kids, not now, not ever. No need to ruin a perfectly wonderful evening with such frivolities, right?

Except these points are not frivolous. It's typically a good idea to remain flexible in your stances, because you never know when they'll change, and when bending on an issue will lead to a greater opportunity or benefit down the line. But bringing such issues up at some early point is vital. It's all too easy for one or both partners to assume they know what's what, when in reality they've been interpreting the words and actions of the other through warped glass.

These intentions needn't be brought up on the first date, but they certainly could be. With everything else you're learning about this person, long-term plans shouldn't be left entirely off the table. Don't allow your future plans to overshadow the potential of "now," however: there's no reason you can't enjoy a date, or a fling, or a full-on relationship with someone who doesn't share your long-term goals. Maintain a flexible stance and communicate about the issues on which you're resolute. With everything on the table, you can enjoy the benefits of both waiting to see what happens *and* having a mutual understanding about what both of you hope to achieve in the future.

Finally, establishing reliable, regular communication habits allows us to keep tabs on changes in ourselves, and in our partners.

This communication needn't be "official" in the sense of sitting down in a conference room and going down a checklist, but it could be. It could also be simply knowing issues will be brought up when they are noticed (see the I'll Tell You Policy), or conversing frequently enough that all cards are on the table, bar none.

This will look different for every relationship, but as long as everyone involved feels they're being heard and aren't in the dark about their partner's thoughts, healthy communication is being achieved.

Far more important than scheduling regular phone calls is ensuring that the line you're using is reliable and clear, and that the language you're speaking is common enough to not require translation.

"THE ONE" POLICY

From a very young age, many of us are told stories about The One: a mystical person who is placed on this planet for us and us alone. It's our "hero's journey" to find this individual, wherever they may be. If pop culture is to be believed, there will be a series of comedic situations and dramatic adventures that lead up to our finding them.

In real life, however, The One is a concept that isn't just irrational, it's potentially harmful. The idea that there's someone out there who is customized to make you whole implies that you're not capable of being complete on your own. It also implies that everyone other than The One is just a stepping-stone toward grand fulfillment, which is a horrible way to approach relationships.

It's understandable why this is such a popular storyline. Who doesn't want to be the hero of the story? Who doesn't want to believe that the imperfections we see in ourselves, and the bad hair days we experience, are just the buildup toward relationship bliss?

The concept of The One actually shares the same history as the concept of a "soul mate," which comes from a tale written by Aristophanes, a comic playwright and contemporary of

Plato. In this particular story, two-headed giants — some with both male and female genitalia, some with two sets of male equipment, and some with pairs of female parts — were sliced down the middle by a jealous Zeus and scattered to the wind. They were doomed forever after to explore the planet, seeking their "other half."

As a metaphor, I get it. And the "soul mate" feeling is one I think most of us are familiar with. That vibe you get from someone who resonates with you is a connection that can be difficult to explain. It's the sum of a huge collection of variables, mental and physical attraction key among them, which add up to something that feels almost metaphysical. It's wonderful and memorable and often more than a little distracting.

To me, reducing something so remarkable to something as kitschy as "magic" or "fate" is borderline offensive. Those feelings are valuable; experiencing them can catalyze some of the most wonderful moments of our lives, and we're supposed to just say, "yeah, it was bound to happen sooner or later"? Why not just celebrate the wonderful coincidences and randomness that brought such a person into your life, instead?

No, it's not magic. And it's not something that can only happen once. Recognizing the shallowness of The One complex allows us to see that we're capable of loving more than a single person in our lifetime.

This is the crux of The One Policy. Why should we limit ourselves when we could be happier more of the time? Why should we be fated to endlessly pursue a fairy tale, when potential sources of *actual* emotional interaction and enjoyment are all around us? Why do we romanticize an idea that couldn't be further from actual romance? An idea that keeps us from experiencing fulfillment, and which forces us to wonder about the legitimacy of our connections with other people when we're fortunate enough to find them?

You are The One. You are the only person in the world who can complete and fulfill you, and ensure your happiness. Everyone else is a potential, hopefully wonderful, addition to that fated situation. You are born complete, you die complete, and you decide whom you spend your time with in between.

ALL OPTIONS POLICY

Let's talk about options.

Within the scope of our relationships, we have options galore. We choose what shape our relationship takes, and how we reshape it over time. We choose who to get involved with, what "involved" means in the context of that coupling, and how much that involvement impacts other aspects of our lives. We choose whether to tether ourselves to someone else in the first place, and if so, how long that tether might be.

The All Options Policy is so-called because it states that all options are on the table. Every possible combination of partners, responsibilities, durations, rules, limits, expectations, and levels of involvement are legitimate, as long as it takes place between consenting adults. This means there are an infinite number of options when it comes to how you communicate, how you relate to one another, how official or unofficial your coupling is by traditional standards, how sex and other forms of physical intimacy play into your relationship, and how your partnership interfaces with other aspects of your life, goals, and ambitions.

The key to understanding this policy is accepting that there's no single moral, upstanding, golden model when it comes to relationships. There are as many valid relationship types as there are people, and it's up to each of us to figure out what unique, specific shape ours will take.

Identifying what we each need and how we might get it plays a major role in how fulfilled and happy we'll be. It also helps us identify potential partners: they either fit within our existing mold, or they make it worth our while to adjust our relationship goals to mesh with theirs.

It can be difficult to see what might be changed and adjusted within or beyond the prototypical, Western, monogamous relationship templates many of us grew up with unless we have some means of comparison. As such, this is a good place to introduce some non-standard relationship frameworks.

Within what's become the traditional monogamous model, two people form a partnership, and that partnership often results in children. This model also includes a menagerie of legal and social norms, ranging from incentives not to hook up with people other than your spouse, which is sometimes legally enforced, sometimes socially, to standards about who does what in the family. Some models, for example, have the male member of a heterosexual couple focusing on his career and making money for the family, while the female partner takes care of the domestic side of things, including, but definitely not limited to, raising the kids.

Now, there's nothing inherently wrong with this model. It's a partnership blueprint that makes sense for a lot of people, and if you're one of them, splendid. You've got fewer big decisions to make on that front. But I would suggest taking a closer look at some of the details to ensure they're tailored to fit you and your partner, and what you want out of life. It may make more sense, for instance, for the female half of an otherwise standard relationship to be work-focused, while the male half stays at home. Or for both partners to be careerists and to either hire someone to help around the house, or to not have kids at all.

You could be involved with someone of the same gender, which throws the traditional gender-role framework out the door. Or you could be involved with more than one partner, allowing for many variations on the traditional theme. Or perhaps you maintain an individual life separate from your partner by not moving in and starting a family, instead opting for something more akin to long-term dating.

This is what I mean when I talk about alternatives to the standard blueprint. There are *many* options out there. Some deviate from the traditional relationship model even more than the examples above, while others are indistinguishable from the typical template in all but one or two specifics.

All of these options, plus any others you might come up with, are legitimate so long as they serve you and your partner's, or partners', needs.

It's valuable to know something about the multitude of relationship types that are out there, because that knowledge allows us to borrow any properties that make sense and cobble them together into a new, "us-shaped" relationship model.

For example, there's a popular relationship model which is often called "ethical non-monogamy," "consensual non-monogamy," or "polyamory." These umbrella labels encompass relationship models in which partners are not incentivized to be physically or emotionally involved with only one person. In polyamorous relationships, for example, each person can have more than one partner, though typically there's a "primary" partner and one or more "secondary" partners. Just as with monogamous relationships, there are limitless variations of this framework, each composed of rearranged bits and pieces from the core idea.

Polyamory isn't for everyone, nor is polyfidelity (having more than one primary partner), open relationships (having multiple relationships, but no partnership hierarchy), or swinging (you and your partner both hooking up with other people, sometimes called "partner swapping"). But regardless of our interest in any specific model, being aware of these options, and knowing that others happily, even gleefully, practice them, gives us permission to more closely examine our own models and to customize them. By recognizing the vast menagerie of options available, and then identifying the extreme ends of that particular spectrum, it's easier to figure out where on the scale you're most comfortable so that you might build something truly fulfilling.

It's possible to be content within almost any model, and to find moments of happiness and fulfillment therein. But it's far more likely that we'll experience intense, ridiculously awesome, lifetime's worth of amazingness if we build our own structures using unique combinations of attributes and guidelines borrowed from other successful relationships.

I should note that some relationship models will be easier to try out and assess than others. For example, jealousy isn't easy to overcome and has been known to complicate things when some people try out aspects of ethical non-monogamy for the first time.

Remember: just because something isn't easy doesn't mean it isn't valuable. I know a lot of people who have taken the time to overcome jealousy and have found incredible fulfillment once they reached the other side. An array of options were suddenly accessible to them thanks to that effort.

On the other hand, just because you overcome something doesn't mean you'll find meaning on the other side. I know folks who have adopted wildly non-standard relationship models and found happiness, but I know just as many who have diligently experimented with their relationships only to find less-common arrangements didn't fulfill them the way a more traditional approach did.

This is the point of the All Options Policy: anything and everything is worth considering, including the model you grew up with. Stay flexible and open, and be willing to try new things when warranted, but don't feel pressured to take an alternative route just because it's trendy or because it makes sense for other people in your life.

This is about finding what's right for *you* and what you want out of life. Let that guide you, and have fun.

FRIENDS FIRST POLICY

The Friends First Policy is just what it sounds like: a commitment to make friendship the foundation of all relationships, be they professional, romantic, or otherwise.

This doesn't necessarily mean that successful relationships need to start out as friendships in order to work. Plenty of people develop friendships with their significant others over time, and that can result in as sturdy a scaffolding as establishing such a bond from the beginning. But it certainly doesn't hurt to lead with that expectation.

One way to ensure this dynamic exists from the beginning is to do away with first dates. Instead, go on coffee dates. What's the difference, you ask? Can't a first date involve coffee?

The distinction lies in the perception of these two concepts. A coffee date can be many things. You could go out with existing friends, clients, or family. Coffee dates are flexible, and imply less.

A first date, on the other hand, comes burdened with all kinds of baggage. Concerns. Expectations. Entire sitcom episodes revolve around first dates, because there are so many details to worry over. Will there be a romantic connection? Will they go in for a kiss at the end? Will this be the day you meet your future spouse? Do you look attractive enough? Would putting more effort into your presentation send the wrong signal? Who's going to pay for the meal? And so on.

Opting for coffee dates alleviates many of these concerns, allowing you to meet someone new, get to know each other, and *then* decide whether there's something worth exploring. Something worth getting all twitterpated about.

If not? You've potentially made a friend, and one who's far more likely to stay that way, because you went out as friends, nothing more. It wasn't a failed date, it was a successful meetup. You enjoyed some coffee, tea, wine, or whatever, and met someone new. Hopefully exchanged at least a few pleasant words, told some stories. The relationship can go any direction from that point, and because of the change in definition, it has a far better chance of survival.

Should things go well in the chemistry department, you now know enough about each other that your next get-together, your first official date, will be all the better for the preparation. Fewer first date jitters and more time spent following up on what you learned the first time around.

In practice, this is unusual. Consider mentioning this policy either before the date when you're initially asking them to get together, or right at the beginning of your meetup, so that the proper tone is set. In my experience, the person on the other side of the conversation visibly relaxes once this distinction is established and the rationale behind it is explained. It's not that people dread dates, or don't want those preordained things to happen, or don't enjoy the process of getting to know someone as a potential "more than friends." It's just that being able to get to know someone as a friend *first* greatly diminishes the potential for massive misunderstanding, pressure, and the need to extricate oneself from a pre-romantic scenario that just isn't working.

You're also more likely to see a "real life" version of the person you're out with, and to be your own, most legitimate self. On a first date, everyone is on their best behavior. If you're just hanging out, even knowing that the next meetup could be a *real* date, you tend to be yourself, as does the other person.

This approach also has future benefits, should things go well and then not so well.

If you're dating someone and you've only ever been romantically involved, there's nothing to fall back on should that title disappear. The result, then, is that a very important person in your life has vanished from it completely and quite suddenly, and it's difficult to swap to another title, like "friend," because you've never had practice being anything but "significant other" to that person.

Starting from friendship allows you to build something valuable and work on it over time; something structurally sound and less brittle than an early, off-the-cuff romantic relationship. Something that could outlast your official, committed partnership.

Breaking up is not easy, regardless of the circumstances. But adopting this policy stacks the deck in favor of being able to stay friends even after your other bonds are gone, which means you get to keep a beloved person in your life while still moving on to someone, or some relationship, that better suits your needs.

As I mentioned above, the latent benefit of "friend dating" over coffee is that even if there's no chemistry, you might end up with a good friend. This means that rather than treating dates as "marriage interviews," you can enjoy yourself, value the person on the other side of the table for whoever they might be, and potentially allow them into your life based on *whichever* role they might fill, rather than only considering the one.

This isn't always possible, of course, since some people can't accept not getting what they wanted out of a date. But if you're able to set expectations early and communicate clearly how things are progressing, they're more likely to go with the flow, and you'll both end up richer for the experience.

As wonderful as it can be to find someone who is "more than a friend," "just friends" can be equally valuable, if not more so. Make that the basis of how you bring people into your life, and dating becomes less about establishing one important relationship in your life, and more about building a series of incredibly worthwhile relationships, each one fulfilling in a different way.

EXIT POLICY

The Exit Policy for relationships is much the same as an exit policy you might have in a hotel: a strategy laid out ahead of time in case of a fire or other dangerous scenario. Applying this same concept to partnerships may sound a little crass, but bear with me on this.

An exit strategy is how you and your partner will respond if the relationship should end. This strategy is optimized to achieve the best possible outcome for you both, all things considered.

This is not a typical relationship discussion topic, but it's an important one. Addressing this scenario *before* it's an issue can be liberating, as it allows you to see that a breakup wouldn't be the end of the world and could be managed in a civil manner. You'll never have to worry that you might make an enemy out of your closest friend, which is knowledge that can strengthen the relationship.

At a fundamental level, this policy ensures you know how to act should things start to crumble. By the time a relationship begins to fall apart, quite often communication channels have already begun to shut down, or at least have become less clear and reliable, and as such the potential for a rational discussion is less likely.

It's easy to shut someone out when you feel they've wronged you, and this frequently becomes a key component of one's survival strategy. As a result, some of us do things that hurt our partners during breakups because little revenges help us cope, even though our coping comes at their expense.

Making a plan of action ahead of time, before any tit-for-tat actions materialize, allows both people to follow a pre-set plan, developed when communication channels were still crystal clear, and when you were just as concerned with ensuring your partner's well-being as your own.

Having an exit strategy makes it easier to give each other space when necessary, mutual support where possible, and to remember that there's a good chance words we don't mean could be said at some point. This allows you to approach an emotional situation more rationally, enabling you to salvage as much as possible from the ashes and maintain your friendship, or at the very least a cordial civility.

Hopefully the plan that results from this policy won't prove necessary, but it's beneficial to plan an exit strategy with your partner even if the risk of your relationship falling to pieces never materializes.

Having this type of discussion shows that you care about keeping your partner in your life, or at the very least not hurting them, *no matter what*. Even in a potential future in which you're no longer together, you're already concerned with their well-being and want to ensure they remain connected to you in some way. I can't think of many things that demonstrate affection as clearly as that sentiment: no matter what, even if we're not together, I want you in my life. I want you to be happy.

Should the relationship end, remember that even if the dynamics between you have changed, the connection is still valuable. Don't throw that value away in favor of the cheap, fleeting feeling of vengeance. Learn the new rules, the new habits, the new "way things are" between you and your ex, and you'll be better off for it.

I'm not going to tell you that breakups are easy, because they seldom are. Even the most prepared, open-minded people experience moments during which the thought of separating just *hurts*, or seems unfair.

That's normal. It's fine. And it doesn't mean you can't spread your arms and gather up the pieces, Lego-like, and start putting them back together again in some brand new shape. It may take time, but it's worth the effort.

There's one post-breakup moment I want to talk about in particular, because it can be immensely challenging to get through, and equally challenging to do so in a way that doesn't risk the "after" you've built with your ex.

When your partner has found someone new, a *new partner*, it can be a make-or-break moment for post-romantic friendships. As such, there are a few specific things worth keeping in mind that may ease the transition.

First, know that this new partner doesn't represent a judgment about you. They aren't better looking than you, they aren't more successful than you; they have nothing to do with you. This is a decision your ex is making based on their current needs or wants. Try to avoid falling into a mental model where you assume every decision they make moving forward somehow relates to you. Chances are, none of them do, negatively or positively. You're not part of that equation, and that's how it should be, because they aren't part of your equation, either.

Second, it can be wonderful to focus on the alliance aspect of your relationship (see the Alliance Policy) with this person, especially right after a breakup. This tends to assuage certain negative, knee-jerk feelings that can crop up, because you're pushing past those reflexes, right into good friend mode. It may not mean giving dating advice, but it could. Flipping the switch to the new normal dilutes the feeling of disconnection from an integral node in your network, because that person is still there; you for them, and they for you.

Finally, take a break if you need it. Don't assume that all of this will just happen overnight. Give it a shot, but if you can't seem to kick your jealousy or post-breakup depression, take some time apart. It helps if you make clear what you're doing from the get-go, so that your actions won't be construed by your ex as you disappearing forever. Just let them know you need some time to adjust, and that you'll talk to them in a month or so. Hide their feeds on your social networks and put the photos from your time together away for a while. Refocus your attention on other things, other people, and you may find that when you reintroduce your ex into your life, they slide more comfortably into a friend role.

Like with all things relationship-related, there are no right or wrong ways to approach the topic of exiting and what happens afterward. One of my relationships ended with a Breakup Party, which my ex and I planned together, inviting all of our friends over to celebrate the end of a wonderful relationship that was in the way of our respective next steps. You needn't do the same, but you *can*.

Dr. Seuss once said, "Don't cry because it's over, smile because it happened." I love that quote, because it's traditional for breakups to be somber affairs, which doesn't do justice to the good times you had, and the lessons you learned. Like a funeral where everyone tells jokes and funny stories to celebrate a life well lived that's come to an end, perhaps your particular relationship deserves a more pleasant seeing-off than sadness or vindictiveness.

When approached this way, the end of a relationship is really just the beginning of a new one: a friendship that has the potential to last well beyond all future romantic engagements. Just remember, this friendship is far more likely to succeed if you lay the groundwork for it ahead of time.

I'LL TELL YOU POLICY

Feeling that you don't know enough about your partner can be stressful and anxiety-inducing. But then, it can be just as bad knowing too much. Or thinking you know too much. Or wondering if you don't know something you should. And so on.

This concern often manifests as worry that your partner is unhappy, or angry at you, or hiding something, or coping with something that's difficult for them and keeping that fact hidden for some unknown reason. Caring and curious, you then try to find out what's wrong, overtly or covertly, so that you might help or otherwise put them at ease.

From there, your partner starts to worry that your worrying means something, or becomes annoyed at what they perceive to be you hassling them or sticking your nose into their business.

The conflict you worried about is therefore started by you worrying about a possible conflict. Self-fulfilling prophecy.

The I'll Tell You Policy is one way to deal with this issue. It's an agreement that if something is wrong, you'll tell your partner. If they agree to do the same, you can both be certain that if something *does* warrant discussion or help, it will be brought up.

If nothing is brought up, that's a reassurance that nothing is the matter, leaving you both free to have a good time. Allowing you to assume that any strange facial expressions they make are just strange, not a sign that they want to break up or have bad news to convey.

This policy, as simple as it is, can take a lot of work to turn into a habit. There will likely be many existing habits that need breaking, and there will be moments where your reflex will be to butt-in and involve yourself in whatever you perceive to be going on in your partner's life.

But it's worth the effort to not do that. Adopting this policy allows all those little tinderbox moments to fly right by. Rather than turning non-issues into points of contention, you can address issues if and when they arise through agreed-upon channels. Rather than reading too much into every fleeting adjustment in vocal tenor, seemingly meaningful look, and deviation from the norm, your partner can relax, confident that things are good until they're told otherwise.

This reduces friction and tension immensely, and prevents those long days wasted worrying over something your partner said or did which they didn't even realize you'd latched onto.

This policy, above all else, is a declaration that you and your partner will be open with each other. That you'll take responsibility for yourselves and communicate your thoughts clearly, rather than assuming responsibility for reading the other's mind.

By saying "I'll tell you if something's wrong," and then actually doing so, you designate every other moment you spend together as "time in which nothing is wrong." To do otherwise is to unintentionally leave those moments undefined, adding stress to stress-less moments and reducing the effectiveness of the "something's up" conversations you *do* have.

ALLIANCE POLICY

As with geopolitics, good relationships depend on reliable, mutually beneficial alliances.

The Alliance Policy states that your partner is your ally. There are two main reasons to view your relationship from this perspective.

The first is that you want your partner to have a stockpile of resources which enables them to better help you achieve your goals, just as you help them achieve theirs. This results in the sharing of information and tools, and the establishment of systems and habits that allow you to support each other effectively. This is true for alliances of any kind.

The second reason to approach your partnership as an alliance is that it creates ties between you and your partner beyond the relationship structure. This means that even if the relationship itself falls apart, you still have reason to stay civil with each other, and even to continue supporting each other in the achievement of your respective goals. You may not be seeing one another in the same sense as before, but as long as you've proven to be helpful and supportive of each other in the past, there will be benefits to working together for mutual gain.

When a relationship ends, the polarity of feelings toward

your partner can flip from positive to negative. Love turns to hate, adoration deteriorates into annoyance, and support warps into something that can resemble obstruction. Hurtful words are said, slanderous stories are told, and tears of both anger and pain are shed. This can be a one-sided attack, or can be a reciprocal conflict. Either way, this is a spiral that can spin out of control, scooping up all the good stuff you wanted to remember and tearing it apart.

Approaching relationships as an alliance, not just as a physical and emotional bond, gives you the excuse to put aside the irrational, vengeful, and hurtful in favor of the practical. It's an excellent way to view someone you care about as not just a romantic partner, but a partner-in-crime. A *confidante*.

There may be situations in which a strong bond cannot be maintained, either because your ex is toxic to your well-being, violent in some way, or otherwise repellent. It's still best to maintain the moral high-ground in this case, but you needn't maintain the partnership by yourself: if the other person isn't carrying their weight, it's no longer a valuable alliance in which to be involved. If the other person is willing and able, though, the benefits of an enduring alliance can be immense.

Adhering to the Alliance Policy means you're committing to having each other's back, no matter what. It means you don't ever want to be enemies, even if the dynamics of your relationship change. It's a state of mind that allows you to invest in a connection that could potentially outlast everything else between you, and even if that should prove unnecessary, it's an indication that you want the core of your partnership to be rock solid. You want them in your life no matter what.

ARGUMENT POLICY

Arguments will happen within relationships. That's probably as close to a given as you can get, without overgeneralizing.

They happen because things don't go the way we'd hoped, or because one partner offends the other. They happen because someone lapsed on a responsibility, or said something in a patronizing tone. Arguments can whip up like sandstorms, and cause nearly as much damage on the interpersonal level because of big things, little things, everything, or nothing. Sometimes they happen for no discernible reason at all: in retrospect you can't remember how it started, only that it did.

It's an easy game to analyze these types of interactions, to pull them apart layer by layer and try to decipher what happened and why. She yelled because he made her feel one way; he walked away because she made him feel another. The "why" of these arguments really aren't what I want to focus on though, because they're going to happen regardless. What's more important is *how* we argue. How we approach arguments, and the role they play in our relationships.

A good policy to consider is that arguments should be discussions. The word "argument" has a messy connotation, because it implies shouting and hurt feelings. A "discussion," on the other hand, is a reasonable discourse between two people trying to reach a conclusion. It may be that one or both arguers is upset or hurt or confused, but rather than shouting or aiming words at their partner's weak spots, they can engage in a discussion to glean information, provide data in return, and attempt to find a solution. Together.

In practice, this means that instead of accusing or otherwise trying to put your partner on their guard, you ask them what's going on from their perspective. Don't interrupt, don't offer any defense, just allow them to speak. Ask questions when they're done, and with as little bias in your voice as possible. Request clarifying information and encourage them to provide it by delaying judgment. Speak calmly, clearly, and without talking down to them; condescension has no place in a discussion.

Then, explain how things seem from your side. Give them information to work with and preface it by saying something like, "From my standpoint, it seemed as if..." Again, avoid placing blame. You're not trying to antagonize or figure out who was more wrong, you're trying to identify the issue and what catalyzed it.

Once you've both had the chance to express your standpoint and hear the other person's point of view, look for a solution or understanding. This means you assess what happened based on the data you both provided. It means you figure out if it was a one-time problem that can be put to rest now that it's been explained, or a longer-term issue that can be prevented in the future by implementing some new policy or mode of operation.

In the latter case, it may be that you sometimes make a face that your partner perceives as being judgmental. After clearly explaining that this is not the case, you should both be able to move forward. Clear communication achieved. On the other hand, it could be that you regularly say things that make them feel small or worthless, in which case you'll want to catch yourself before saying such things in the future. Commit to making the effort, and then actually make that effort.

It's remarkable how few conflicts arise after a few tense situations have been defused by discussions of this kind. You'll find that you can both assume, with good reason, that your partner isn't going to do anything to hurt you. And you'll know that if some issue *does* come up, it will be a problem you can simply and rationally handle, together.

This approach to arguing is vital to the larger practice of being civil within relationships. In all things, aspire to maintain a civil stance toward your partner. During arguments, awkward moments, breakups, or anything else that would typically rile you up, default to civility. Be calm. Be friendly and kind, even when you're not particularly feeling that way.

If ever there comes an argument where one person wins and the other loses, both people have lost. A relationship is weakened if there's ever only one winner, because you're a team working together to build something great. A loss for one is a loss for you both.

CAMPSITE POLICY

The Campsite Policy is based on the "campsite rule" that was coined by advice columnist Dan Savage as advice for folks who are dating someone much younger or less experienced than themselves. When camping, you clean up after yourself before you leave and try to avoid leaving your campsite a mess for the next person who camps there. The campsite rule says that it's fine to date someone who is at a different point in their life, as long as you leave them at *least* as happy and healthy as you found them, and ideally, even better.

The Campsite Policy takes that concept a little further to encompass all relationships. We all hold some kind of power over our partner when we're in a relationship, whether that power is overt or covert. As a result, it makes sense that we should try to wield that power benevolently.

Rather than leaving a trail of emotionally broken people in our wake, used up and developmentally stagnant, *everyone* is better off if we actively help our partners grow.

We benefit from this policy because we get to enjoy the company of a maturing partner; someone who gets better and better each day. Those who might date us or our partners at some point in the future benefit because they'll be enjoying the company of a wonderful person who was partially shaped by the dynamics of a previous, excellent relationship. Our partners benefit because they have had a positive, growth-oriented experience with someone who treated them well and didn't saddle them with emotional or physical baggage.

The importance of making growth a default within a relationship cannot be overstated. All too often change is unintentionally stifled by well-meaning people who don't want their partner to face difficulty or harm. By helping them pursue their passions and reach their goals, you're contributing to their overall, long-term happiness, potentially even beyond the duration of the relationship.

People can be damaged by relationships, especially when their couplings are defined by an imbalance of power, a lack of clear communication that results in misunderstandings and heartache, or when the relationship end with a dramatic breakup.

The Campsite Policy is an approach to relationships which asks that we never lose sight of the bigger picture. It helps us remember that our partners are human beings beyond the place and time in which we intersect with them, and that it's our responsibility to do our best to ensure they're happy and healthy as long as it's within our power to do so.

SPACE, SILENCE, PRIVACY POLICY

Imagine a couple enjoying their relationship. Chances are you pictured them cuddled up on the couch, necking in a theater, or maybe holding hands, walking through a carnival where one has obtained a massive stuffed animal for the other.

These are wonderful relationship-related activities, but I would argue that the less screen-worthy shared moments tend to be the real glue: the stuff that holds everything else together. Because although there will be times where you're connected at the hip, and there will be times where you can't get enough of each other, the rest of the time you'll be trying to live your life and balance the presence and needs of someone else with your own. Those who strike this balance tend to have happy, drama-free partnerships. Those who don't are likely to burn out and end things prematurely.

Three oft-underrated values lend their names to this policy: space, silence, and privacy. Each is important for a slightly different reason and can be difficult to integrate or improve upon without a little effort.

Having space in a relationship means that you're able to get time alone. It means being able to tuck away somewhere and read without being distracted by someone who is, let's be honest, quite distracting for many wonderful reasons. It means being able to focus on your lifestyle choices: taking quiet walks, surfing the Internet, and having your own friends, independent of the relationship. It means being able to focus on your career and your hobbies.

"Space" can also mean physical space, whether it's a separate room, a partitioned-off area, or even just a coffee shop where you can be alone in public. Having space in a relationship, as much as you need of it, balances your couple-to-individual ratio so that you're able to be a wonderful singular person, as well as an enthusiastic part of something larger with someone you care about.

Silence is a bit like space, but occurs while you're together. There's something incredibly romantic about being with someone without having to say a word. To be comfortable in the same room, or even snuggled up on a couch, but still off in your own world, doing your own thing.

I often picture an older married couple when I think about the capacity for silence in a relationship. Two people sitting in their own rocking chairs in front of a nice, warm fire, one reading a book, the other reading the paper, and both smiling with the satisfaction of having someone they care about nearby while enjoying individual activities and thoughts.

Many people find silence difficult because they assume that if they can't keep their partner entertained or engaged at all times, something is wrong. This couldn't be further from the truth, so long as both people understand that silence is a means of being alone together, not a communication breakdown.

Having privacy within a relationship doesn't mean actively keeping important information from one another, but rather having personal space, thoughts, projects, or whatever else one might want to keep to oneself. It means being able to have conversations with friends without your partner growing concerned or jealous; it means being able to have relationships with people outside your partnership without the necessity for oversight.

An expectation of privacy is a good indication of confidence within the relationship. It shows trust, on both sides, and so long as vital data isn't being kept from your partner (say, that your STD test came back positive, or that you're planning on moving to another country at the end of the month), there's no reason why every single detail of what you're up to has to be made available to them. There's no reason why your journal should be open-access, or why you should worry that your partner will dig through your text messages. Invasive activities of that kind show a lack of confidence, and should probably either be addressed directly to ascertain why they feel so self-conscious (or why you do, if you're the one snooping), or taken as a sign that perhaps you should be seeing other people.

In aggregate, the three concepts that make up the Space, Silence, Privacy Policy allow people in a relationship to demonstrate trust, have lives outside of the partnership, and be comfortable with their partner, without feeling the need to put on a show every moment of every day.

NEEDS AND LIMITS POLICY

If you want to find fulfillment with another person, an ideal first step is to become personally, independently fulfilled.

Depending on someone else to bring happiness to your life, zest to your day-to-day, and inspiration to your work, is handing off a *lot* of responsibility; it's depending on your partner to make you complete.

If you're happy, inspired by a wide variety of things, driven by your work, surrounded by creative catalysts, and confident in yourself, you're more likely to make rational choices about who a potential partner *actually* is and what they add to your life. That is to say, you'll make choices based on preference, not desperation.

Ideally, you're not drowning. Ideally, you're able to choose whom you bring into your life based on the joy they add to it, not out of some kind of survival instinct. But that's a tall order if you don't know what fulfills you.

Determining who you are and what you want, while also keeping tabs on how far you're willing to push in the pursuit of greater happiness and fulfillment, for you *and* for your partner, is the focus of the Needs and Limits Policy.

If you don't know or understand your needs, your wants,

your strengths and weaknesses, you're far less capable of finding someone who's a glorious addition to your world. You'll be more likely to settle for someone who merely "completes" something that felt incomplete before.

Regardless of what kind of relationship you're looking for, it's more practical to be a whole person, yourself, rather than looking for someone to make you whole. You don't want to be a fraction, looking for another fraction. You want to be a complete person looking for the same, which leads to much more favorable math. When two complete people are added together, one plus one equals three. You're both better for being together.

You can be complete and still value relationships. But doing so requires that you figure out who you are, build upon that knowledge, and bring people into your life as it makes sense, not as a panicked reflex.

Given the option, most people would rather partner with someone who can carry their own weight and have extra strength left to share than with someone who needs to be carried every step of the way. Approaching relationships in this fashion has the added benefit of making you even more of a catch.

Just as you're better off knowing, understanding, and acting upon your own needs, it's likewise beneficial to become familiar with your partner's needs. Doing so allows you to help them achieve their ends while they do the same for you.

It's important to note that just because your partner has a need doesn't mean it's your responsibility to fulfill it. It's possible that they will want something that you cannot or will not play a role in, which warrants a conversation as to how you'll move forward knowing what you now know about each other's needs and limits.

In most cases there will be room for flexibility. Even if their needs push up against your limits, you'll likely be able to come up with a compromise that serves you both, so long as you can each bend a little on the details. This can strengthen the relationship, and allow for safe, consensual experimentation.

However, some needs, no matter how much they complete us and how simply they might be fulfilled, will be unfulfillable by your partner. It sucks when this happens, whether it's because the need itself is a tricky one, because your partner isn't willing to find a middle ground, or because you're unwilling or unable to find an alternative to achieving the same end.

There are three main options in such circumstances, and none of them are straightforward.

The first is to keep negotiating, communicating, hoping and praying, and chipping away at whatever it is that's keeping this need of yours unfulfilled. It may take days, weeks, years, it may never happen, but you can stick with it nonetheless. Who knows? It may be that your partner changes their mind; or maybe you'll change yours. Or perhaps one or both of you will evolve into different versions of yourselves, so that the need is no longer necessary, or is no longer unfulfillable.

The second option is to break up. This is obviously non-ideal, but it's also an excellent and very rational option if what you need is vital and you're not getting it. If you've expressed the importance of your need and worked with your partner to make it happen, and there's still no movement in the right direction, your best bet may be to pick up your ball and go home. Stay on good terms, but start looking for someone else to play with.

The third option, and the one that's perhaps the least typical, would be to find someone else who can fulfill this need of yours while staying with your partner. It may be that you need a partner to exercise with, or want someone who you can talk to about your day. Finding a workout buddy or someone to talk to wouldn't be a wildly unorthodox move, and it would allow your relationship to continue unabated. Finding a stand-in could be a little less typical if the need is something more intimate: wanting someone who will tie you up during sex, for instance, or someone who will help you work through dark memories that keep coming to mind.

This third option, though non-standard, is worth considering. It can allow everyone involved to get what they need without burdening any single person with unreasonable expectations. It would mean not having to find one person who checks every box in terms of what you're looking for in a partner.

Of course, there are plenty of reasons why many people wouldn't opt for this third option: jealousy, potential safety issues, emotional complications, and even just the logistics of it all. Perceived social drawbacks, too, keep people from investigating multi-partner options. Societal and social norms rest upon the archetypical one-for-one style relationship, and anything that colors outside those lines can be perceived as being wrong or dangerous, even if they're typically not; at least not when entered into for the right reasons, with respect for all involved, and a good dose of responsibility.

Whether approached in a standard or an outside-the-box way, identifying and knowing your needs, and those of your partner, are key components of successful relationships. Get these figured out and addressed, and there will be fewer catalysts for unhappiness in your couplings.

In addition to your own needs, ideally you're aware of and flexible in helping achieve your partner's needs. An enthusiastic "we're in this together, let's make sure we're both taken care of and supported" mentality ensures that everyone is able to pursue happiness in their own way, knowing that their partner is in their corner no matter what. Independent realization, then, becomes a group effort. You're both better off for having the other around, while still being strong individually.

But everyone has limits when it comes to fulfilling the needs of others, whether those limits are close at hand or far off in the distance. It may be that you've yet to hit such a ceiling, and your no-go zone is theoretical rather than tangible. But it's good to know that, should you ever be put in an uncomfortable position or discover a new limit, your partner will recognize this and not demand its removal.

This is not to say that perimeters can't be bypassed and restraints can't be broken. I would argue that most successful relationships involve the challenging of limits, and doing so in a supportive environment where you know you've got backup.

That being said, another person demanding that you ignore your limits is not okay. So long as you're communicative about this frontier of yours, there's no excuse for them to pressure you into going beyond it if you're not keen to do so.

This can be tricky because it requires that you know the shape and location of your limits pretty well, and can clearly communicate what scares you, what stirs up bad feelings from the past, what you're not comfortable doing sexually, and what you don't want to discuss for whatever reason. Often you have to encounter these limits before you know they exist, so if you're not careful, it may come as a shock to your partner when a barrier springs up seemingly out of nowhere.

This is why it's valuable to be comfortable talking about your wills and will nots with your partner. It means that, if and when you're caught off guard by your own hesitation or a just-discovered limit, you're capable of figuring out that it's not flying that scares you, but being cooped up in a confined space. It's not sex that scares you, it's being naked in front of another human being. They won't always be able to help you deal with your limits directly, but they'll be there to support you in whatever way they can, regardless.

Expecting someone else to respect your limitations is not too much to ask, but it does mean that you have to respect theirs, too. Again, this doesn't mean that you have to walk on eggshells around your partner, worried that you might step over some invisible line and ruin everything. But it does mean having a reliable and clear channel of communication so they can tell you when a line has been reached. It means establishing trust so that if one of their lines is crossed unintentionally, you can step back together and assess what happened, identify the issue, and figure out what to do next; whether that means erasing or bending the line, or exploring elsewhere instead.

Why this focus on limits to begin with?

There's no right or wrong way to interact with someone, and no right or wrong way to connect with them and experience a deeper "closeness." But more options mean more ways to express and experience this deep connection. The reluctance you feel when getting close to someone, then, might be worth working on. Not because you can't have healthy relationships without doing so, but because limits diminish your number of options; having fewer of them tends to be more ideal.

Do not be defined by your limitations. Allowing yourself to be thus defined impacts not just you, but everyone you have a relationship with. It sullies many aspects of the connections we have with others, influences how we view ourselves, and restricts how we allow ourselves to interact with the world.

Starting now, allow your limitations to be bendable, even breakable. Know that you can reshape them however you see fit, individually or with the help of a trusted partner.

ARCHETYPE POLICY

Don't try to force a person to be someone they're not. This is the crux of the Archetype Policy.

To get more specific, don't pressure yourself, or your partner, to be an archetypical anything; an archetypical husband, an archetypical girlfriend, an archetype of their gender or faith or race or upbringing. This cookie-cuttering is something that happens with alarming frequency within relationships, and it's the cause of much conflict between people who otherwise adore each other.

Let's start with self-archetyping. We're given examples of people to emulate from a young age, and this generally means being presented with role models who represent a certain ideal to our parents, educators, older siblings, or someone else with influence over our growth. The result is that we grow up with a notion about the "correct" way to act, and this carries over into how we behave in the context of a relationship.

The same thing tends to happen outwardly. We meet someone, are attracted to something about them, but then feel the need to fix just a few things here and there. Fixer-uppers, they're sometimes jokingly called. Good people, but they'll need a little tuning up before they make an ideal mate.

When it comes to relationships, opting for a "fixer-upper" tends to be a recipe for disappointment. It also represents more than a little arrogance on the part of the person planning to do the fixing.

Finding someone you intend to change means you've decided that who they are, what they want, and how they live is inferior to who you are, what you want, and how you live. Their goals are not as awesome as your goals. Their habits and hobbies don't live up to yours. They are ramshackle, and you will refurbish them.

But implicit superiority complex aside, approaching relationships in this way means you're partnering with someone who you consider to be a block of raw material that you can chisel into whatever shape you prefer. You want to whittle away who they are so that they become the person you want them to be, or whom you *feel* you should want them to be. This typically results in negative complexes and disappointment on both ends.

A more ideal path would be to know what type of person you want in your life, get off your ass, and *find* them. Put some effort into it, learn something about yourself along the way, and be open to changing your mind as you encounter different types of people. Because a trait that commonly comes tandem with the desire to mold an ideal partner is a lack of experience with people; experience that might teach you that looking for a fixer-upper is a bad idea to begin with, and that *everyone* in a relationship has the opportunity to evolve, but in a natural, non-forced, non-harmful way.

This is not to say that encouragement and growth have no place in a relationship: on the contrary, most healthy relationships have such a system built-in, through which both partners achieve bigger, better things over time.

The difference is that in healthy relationships those ambitions aren't forced or guilted upon anyone; they're goals that the pursuer truly desires, not goals they feel compelled to chase in order to keep their partner happy, or to keep their relationship from falling apart.

Don't seek fixer-uppers, seek people who make you happy and with whom you can grow.

The same applies to you and the perception you have of yourself. Considering *yourself* a fixer-upper, with the ultimate goal of achieving someone else's standards, is a great way to be disappointed.

Don't try to become someone else's ideal archetype: be *you*. Be so wonderfully you that new archetypes are created in your image. And allow your partner the same freedom.

STRESS TEST POLICY

You don't want to wait to stress test your relationships. If you do, you may find yourself depending on that relationship, only to find it's changed in some way overnight, like a sweater that has shrunk in the dryer, leaving you chilly and without alternative wardrobe options at a pivotal moment.

Preventing this suboptimal situation is the purpose of the Stress Test Policy. It says that you shouldn't be gentle when figuring out what your relationship is, who plays which roles, and how everyone involved interacts.

We all like to put our best foot forward when going out with someone who doesn't yet know us well, but there's a difference between amplifying who we *actually* are and pretending to be someone else. No one benefits if you falsely represent yourself, only to pull back the curtain months later, finally revealing the shrunken-sweater truth. This is not constructive, and it's not kind.

Playing false is a manifestation of a lack of self-confidence. You should own who you are, proudly display your true colors, and wait to see how the other person responds. If you're into musicals and your partner is not, you needn't rub it in their face, but you shouldn't have to hide that side of yourself for their benefit. If they can't tolerate you enjoying something they don't, they're probably not worth pursuing. The same is true for sexual preferences, expectations about relationship dynamics, how a person views the world, and just about everything else. You needn't sync up at every turn, but feeling the need to hide something important about yourself shows that you think there might be conflict as a result. That's no way to live.

Similarly, it's important to be open and honest with your partner in figuring out who *they* are. If unfamiliar facets of their personality emerge, ask them about these uncharted aspects of who they are. Respond positively and with an open mind. It may be that they're changing, or trying out something new, or it may be that they're starting to trust you more; that they have grown comfortable enough to stress test you, and they didn't feel confident doing so previously.

An excellent way to stress test a relationship thoroughly and intensely is by traveling with your partner.

Travel is, above all else, an imperfect experience. If you over-plan or require every moment to align with the spreadsheet schedule you prepared, you'll be in for a major let-down when the landing gear hits the tarmac and you find yourself without your luggage, suffering from food poisoning, or unable to stay in the room with East-facing windows you had booked.

This is what makes travel so useful in the context of relationships. Life isn't always going to go according to plan, and if you can stand your partner under the most trying of circumstances — like when a camel spits on their only suit jacket, or when you discover there's no hot water available in your hostel — your relationship is more likely to have staying power, even through life's most difficult moments.

Of course, the travel experience is also a means of figuring out how you interact with each other away from your safe, cozy, habitual environment. Being extracted from the familiarity of home changes the dynamics between people and can alter how we interact with the world. Someone who's usually more of a go-with-the-flow type might transform into a domineering Type-A while in transit, while the person who's large and in charge and makes all the decisions in a familiar environment may take the back seat for a while, content to follow rather than lead.

Even if you're not overly fond of travel and don't plan to make it an integral part of your lifestyle, taking a few trips with your partner can help you understand how you both plan, improvise, deal with new ideas and ways of life, cope with uncomfortable situations, and spend money while away from your default routines.

Travel, in short, is a compressed, microcosm of life. It's a relatively small investment of time and money that allows you to gaze into the future and learn something valuable about a person with whom you may be spending a great deal of time. It's one of many ways to stretch and wash that sweater to see how well it survives the realities of life *before* it becomes too integral to your wardrobe.

SEX POLICY

Sex can be a wonderful thing. It floods your body with happiness-inducing chemicals, it's a pretty decent workout, and I've heard it can even help you make a child, if you're into that kind of thing.

It's also an excellent way to connect with another person, though the Sex Policy is all about separating the *act* of sex from the *meaning* of sex in our relationships. Let me tell you why.

Sex is a great way to connect with another person, but it's not the *only* way to connect. Building it up as the be-all, end-all method of mind-melding with someone does a grave injustice to all the other means we have available: a smile, a hug, a conversation. This perception also risks of stripping sex of all but one of its valuable attributes. If sex is reduced to "making love" in the sense that it's a way to connect and only a way to connect, you miss out on how much fun it can be. Something you do with someone you like, certainly, but perhaps because you're randy, not because you're trying to show them how much you care about them. Sex allows for strong connections, but it can be so much more than that, too, and using it as a means of showing affection and nothing else is dismissing all but one of its potential benefits.

Also consider that there are many, many ways to connect with another person, and sex needn't be one of them for a relationship to be legitimate and intense. Some relationships are intimate without ever becoming sexual, closeness being all that's needed to bond with the other person, whether physical or intellectual, and that can weave a connection that's just as genuine and valuable as one that culminates in sex.

This policy is not about belittling the role of sex, but removing it from an apex position within a relationship. It's about removing the aura of primacy from sex so that it can be enjoyed for whatever it needs to be in the moment, and for the people involved, whether that means enjoying the act of sex is the only thing you have in common with your partner, or whether it's more often something you do to communicate a certain sentiment or emotion. Or perhaps even something you never do at all.

Separating sex from the relationship means we're freer to experience intense connections in an infinite number of ways, not just the one. It also means we can enjoy sex beyond its oft-implied role as a wedding ring accompaniment; it's not a step on the way to something else, it can be a purpose unto itself. It means we're more liberated to push limits and see what really makes us feel alive, both in the relationships we build and in the sex we have.

JEALOUSY POLICY

Jealousy is not a fact of life, nor the sign of a healthy relationship. It's not beneficial or romantic. It's not warranted.

Jealousy is instinctual to many people, though these instincts, like so many others we act upon, are not conducive to living happily in modern, civil society. Just like the instinct that suggests we should have sex with anything that looks appealing, and the one that would have us gobbling up any food left unguarded, so too is it worthwhile to extract ourselves from the influence of the jealousy complex.

For some, this is an easy task. Some people don't feel possessive of others, or regard a smile from their partner aimed at another person as a potential threat to their own position in the relationship. For most, though, disentangling ourselves from jealousy takes some effort. Perhaps a lot of effort.

There are a multitude of variables that determine where you reside on the jealousy scale: some cultures have more historical acceptance of jealous feelings and actions than others, for example. Some individuals, too, seem more predisposed to be jealous, no doubt due to a combination of nature and nurture.

Origins of these feelings aside, jealousy is a pox upon civil discourse and rational partnership. A jealous person is covetous and envious, upset by innocuous looks and interactions. It's something we're prone to justify, especially those of us who feel jealousy on a deep level, because it seems like something that just *is*.

But we *can* get rid of it, with some effort. The idea that we can't do anything about jealousy and that it's somehow indomitable is merely a convenient excuse for not trying to do anything about it: similar excuses are used by people who want to get fit but refuse to change their diet and never set foot in a gym.

Life without jealousy is worth aspiring to, and that's what this policy is all about. Jealousy, at its core, is about feeling threatened. It's a response to worrying that your partner will leave you, or that you're not good enough, or that you're not getting a balanced return on what you're investing in the relationship. In order to start moving away from jealousy, it's best to start with the causes of these feelings.

An excellent first step is to notice your feelings and figure out where they originate. If you're feeling a little down today, why do you think that is? What did you do differently that might have caused that feeling? What did you eat? Did you skip a workout, or workout differently? Was there an interaction that might have caused the shift in mood?

This type of regular assessment gives you a means of ascertaining which feelings are caused by easily controlled variables, like diet, and which are the result of interactions and your interpretation of those interactions.

If you find that your mood is being impacted by external factors, like your significant other seemingly flirting with your friend, rationally evaluating the event allows you to either push the moment aside as unimportant, or address it in order to bring about closure.

In the above example, this would mean looking at the context in which this supposed flirting occurred. Were you standing right there next to them when it happened? Was it really flirting, or was it just being playful and friendly? Has this kind of maybe-flirting resulted in anything negative with this partner in the past? If there was flirting involved, does it matter? Does it bug you enough to warrant drama or a potential breakup?

In most cases, pulling the scenario apart in this way will show that your brain was sending you warning signals that weren't applicable, and what happened wasn't actually anything worth your worry. It was a misinterpretation, or a gut-reaction that didn't actually make sense after you thought about it, or you misunderstood the context.

In some cases, rationally deconstructing something like this will allow you to clearly explain the situation to your partner so as to keep it from happening again in the future. Going back to the previous example, it could be that someone cheated on you in the past and you're therefore extra-sensitive to anything that seems to be headed in that direction. Your best bet, then, may be to tell your partner about that still-tender bruise in your history so that if you do misinterpret something in the future, they'll understand why. This also allows them to change their mannerisms in some way, if warranted, to avoid setting off that warning bell again in the future. In this way, you work together to short-circuit negative feelings that could result from your partner's actions.

Solving this problem isn't all on them, though. If they're willing to adjust their actions to help, that's wonderful, but if there's no reason to believe there's an actual issue and you're behaving irrationally, that's on you. Recognize when this is the case, pull the situation apart as mentioned above, and remember that jealousy is self-consciousness in action and not something you want or need. Be aware of what's happening and act with intention. Push the jealous feelings aside and get back to enjoying your relationship.

Rational analysis is the bane of irrational, jealous feelings, and it's worth becoming familiar with this technique so that fewer scenarios result in drama.

That being said, if you find yourself in a relationship that fires up your jealousy response no matter how you try to stifle it, consider finding a new partner who doesn't keep you stewing in a jealous rage all the time.

BUILD UP POLICY

It may sound trivial, but snide, cutting jokes aimed at your partner can take a toll. It's death by a thousand papercuts: each individual nick seems small and insignificant, and may not even be noticed. But in aggregate? They can maim or kill a relationship.

It's not just jokes with a critical angle that can be harmful, but anything you do that has a negative undertone. Joking about your partner's weight or intelligence. Implications that you're putting up with them in some way, or holding out for someone better. Even criticism that is meant to encourage your partner to reach new heights can have this effect. They can build up in the blood over time, eventually reaching toxic levels.

The Build Up Policy is all about building your partner up rather than breaking them down. It's possible to be funny and joke around without being negative. It's possible to positively reinforce behavior you'd like to see more of, rather than negatively reinforcing with criticism or meanness. It's possible to maintain an uplifting, inspiring, encouraging vibe all the time, even when things are looking grim or the relationship is on the rocks.

This policy is about more than simply not hurting someone

you care about, it's also about helping to build your partner up so they feel more confident and capable. It creates an always-on support system that makes them feel buoyed by your presence, not weighed down by it. It ensures you're the person they'll want to share their successes with, and with whom they'll want to confide their goals and concerns. It allows them to feel comfortable with you, rather than concerned about what you're going to say next. It shows that you're someone who will provide a helping hand up, not someone who will slap them down.

CHEATING POLICY

The concept of cheating within a relationship can seem complicated, but this policy is a simple one.

Cheating, for the purposes of this book, is breaking the rules of your relationship. Different relationships have different rules, and as such none are set in stone or applicable to every relationship.

That being said, every relationship has rules, whether they're explicit or implicit. Some will be addressed concretely in conversation, while others will be assumed.

Assuming, by the way, is a bad idea, and runs opposite to the purpose of the Cheating Policy. This policy states that you should get everything on the table as soon as possible: the rules, expectations, and consequences for the violation of this informal contract. If you are uncertain as to the specifics of a rule, either because you didn't fully understand it or because it was never covered, ask before potentially breaking that rule.

Now, it's important to remember that you'll always have the option to cheat. This is a given for any situation in which there are rules by which you're expected to abide. But I would argue that cheating is a bad idea even if you feel the guidelines of your relationship are somehow unfair, unjust, or don't jive with your worldview.

Cheating hurts someone you care about and is a means of trying to get something you want without dealing with the repercussions of your actions. If you want to date other people, end your monogamous relationship first. If you want to date multiple people on a regular basis, stop doing the monogamous thing and adopt a relationship style that is a better fit for your needs (like polyamory or open relationships). You can even have a conversation with your current partner and see about adjusting the rules in some way; you never know, maybe they'd like to explore a bit, too, while still maintaining what you've got.

Cheating, however, is the coward's approach to fulfillment. It's an incredibly short-term play in a scenario that calls for long-term thinking. There are plenty of ways for you to get what you want from your relationships, and cheating is the worst option of all, right down there at the bottom, alongside staying in a relationship that's making you miserable.

This policy is as much about being real with yourself as it is about not hurting your partner. If you're cheating and telling yourself that there's nothing wrong with your relationship, you're harboring some serious delusions.

Rules in relationships exist for a reason: to provide safety and a sense of security for those involved. Break those rules and you're putting yourself and those you care about at risk, and fostering insecurity in both yourself and your partner.

Be honest with yourself and don't hurt those you care about. Adhere to the rules you've agreed to, or find a situation with rules that better suit your needs.

INTENTIONAL OPENING POLICY

There are times when you should leave your partner well enough alone. Times when misreading a situation can create a problem where there wasn't one (see the I'll Tell You Policy). Not all glances are meaningful, not all silences pregnant with unspoken words.

In some cases, though, awkwardness *is* meaningful, and it's worth learning to make the distinction.

A good rule of thumb is that if your partner drops hints, starts to bring something up but doesn't fully commit, or frequently leads back to the same topic, it may be something they're trying to address but aren't sure how to, yet. You can help them get there, though perhaps asymmetrically.

For example, if your partner mentions feeling a little out of shape three times over the span of a couple of days. Rather than saying, "Why don't you just work out, then?" and potentially sparking a heated discussion out of nothing, accidentally offending them, or ignoring the issue outright, you could take a softer approach. You could test the waters with something like, "I've been thinking about trying out a different workout routine for a month and seeing how I like it." An opening like this brings the topic to the forefront of conversation without accusing or judging. It brings the topic up invitingly, and allows your partner to use the opening or not, depending on whether there really *was* something they wanted to discuss.

If they *don't* take the opportunity, you can be more certain there's nothing to worry about and drop the issue. But if there *is* something they want to discuss, and they either haven't been able to figure out how to bring it up thus far or hadn't fully realized it was bugging them, you've just provided them with a well-paved path toward that goal.

It's a good idea to remember, too, that not all concerns or topics of discussion are requests for a solution. Sometimes, your partner may simply want to vent about work or muse about politics. Leaving an intentional opening can catalyze these sorts of conversations, as well, allowing them to let off steam more easily, without feeling that they're burdening you with information or stories you're not interested in hearing about.

Whatever the case, providing subtle conversational openings can help keep communication channels open, which can help maintain the overall quality of your relationships.

CASUAL ROMANCE POLICY

The word "romance" means something different to everyone who hears it, much like the word "love."

As such, my concept of romance will no doubt be different from yours, and when your partner puts in the effort to be romantic, it may not register as anything special to you.

The Casual Romance Policy is an effort to acknowledge and cope with this interpretive minefield. It says, in essence, that romance should be a day-to-day thing, rather than a one-day-out-of-the-year thing. Instead of being something you do while trying to get laid, or something you do when trying to get off the hook for a misstep, or some kind of upkeep you pay in order to keep things peaceful around the house, romance should be part of your everyday experience. It gets baked into how you interact, making even the most mundane situations interesting and fun and potentially titillating.

In practice, this means learning enough about your partner that you can figure out what makes them feel special, makes them feel loved, turns them on, and sends a jolt of happiness through their bodies.

The tricky aspect of this policy is that most of us have shortcut answers to the question "What do you find romantic?"

and you often have to dig a little deeper to figure out the core of the answer given.

Imagine you're dating someone who absolutely loves getting flowers. Giving them a bouquet makes their day. You could try to give them flowers every day, but that would become old and expected (and expensive) at some point, and flowers are probably just one manifestation of some larger enthusiasm, anyway.

That core enthusiasm is what you're looking for. Maybe it's not just flowers that they like, but tangible displays of your affection. Another aesthetically pleasing gift, then, might garner the same, or better, results. Perhaps they enjoy the traditional aspect of giving flowers: opening doors and pulling out chairs, then, might be a casual way to bring romance into their day-to-day experience. Maybe it's less about the flowers and more about a clearly communicated message: I care about you, and I went out of my way to get you this object that expresses as much. It could be that simply expressing your feelings more clearly is the key. Instead of assuming that they know how you feel, occasionally say something like "You really are amazing," or "Thanks for being with me tonight," or "Goddamn you're sexy." Something, anything, that shows them they're cared for.

The specifics will be different in every case, but that's the idea: to make each moment more meaningful by periodically underlining it with something expressive, unexpected, or joy-inducing. It's not a matter of trying to make every moment a parade, or buying happiness, or being uncharacteristically sentimental. It's about trying to increase the level of happiness your partner feels by amplifying what's already there, and doing so consistently.

You can choose to be anywhere in the world, with anyone you want to be with, and you choose to be *there*, with *them*.

Express that, and enjoy the choice that you've made while helping them do the same.

HAPPINESS POLICY

Happiness is subjective. As you grow and change, so do your needs and wants, and the things that once made you happy may not anymore, making room for new joy-inducing things.

The Happiness Policy says that this subjectivity is just fine, and that you won't make decisions based on an outdated standard.

For example, you may remember your first relationship being the most magnificent thing ever. You were never more in love, the sex was the best you've ever had, your partner was the most caring, kind, loving person you've ever dated. This may actually be the case, but there's a decent chance that you're making an unfair comparison because of a previous lack of context. Your first partner had no one else to compete with, you had no basis for comparison as to what that kind of love felt like and how good sex could be, and as such they were being held up to very different standards than someone you might date today. Today, you have the benefit of vastly more perspective about the world, relationships, yourself, and what you want. If you were to have that same relationship today, you'd very likely wonder what all the fuss was about; you have wildly different standards now.

This is not to belittle the value of that first relationship, and that's key to this policy. Recognizing that happiness is subjective and that different things evoke it over time means that you're better able to assess which things make you happy in a given context. That first relationship? Perfect for you at the time. It made you very happy then, and that's valuable, even if it wouldn't do much for the modern iteration of you.

Similarly, the "you" of this moment should judge relationships based on who you are *now* and what you want *today*, not standards made up by someone else, standards developed by you at a very different time in your life, or standards that you think may apply to you at some point in the future. Allow your happiness to be *now-centric* and enjoy it.

This policy helps alleviate the issue of judging all future relationships by the standards and risks and payoffs of the past. This is often called "baggage," and the baggage in this case is us hauling around all these preconceived notions about who we are, how our interactions with other people need to be or will be, and what that other person's motivations are. This is unfair to us, our partner, and the relationship. It's also limiting as hell and based on fear: a fear that we'll be caught unprepared, or won't have learned from the past.

Ideally we do learn from the past and use it to shape new scenarios, rather than as an excuse to repeat old mistakes, dream about old successes, and passively accept the same relationships and storylines over and over again, forever.

Allow yourself to evolve between relationships, and allow yourself, your partner, and the dynamics of your relationship to change during your time together, too.

Don't force something that isn't there; embrace what *is*. Stay malleable rather than rigid and fragile, and you'll continue to develop increasingly higher standards while also enjoying each experience on its own merit.

OUTRO

There's no right or wrong way to approach relationships, but there are paths that will help you grow with your partner, and paths that will stifle growth. There are approaches that favor short-term benefits over long-term well-being, and those that lead to an inherent imbalance, resulting in instability and discontent.

Whatever your priorities, whoever you are, and whichever people you're fortunate enough to bring into your life, for a time, or forever, remember that healthy relationships start with *you*. They start with your own level of self-confidence, your individual ability to be present and committed to growth, and your personal dedication to be a net-positive for the world; to be someone who adds to the lives of others, rather than sapping them of joy and momentum.

Your most intimate relationship is, and should always be, with yourself. Acknowledge and maintain that foundation, then reach out into the world and help others do the same. Ensure that your sense of "me" is mighty so that your sense of "we" can follow suit.

ABOUT THE AUTHOR

Colin Wright is an author, entrepreneur, and full-time traveler. He was born in 1985 and lives in a new country every four months; the country is voted on by his readers. More info at colin.io.

ALSO BY COLIN WRIGHT

CONNECT WITH COLIN ONLINE

Blog
Exilelifestyle.com

Work
Colin.io

Twitter
Twitter.com/colinismyname

Facebook
Facebook.com/colinwright

Instagram
Instagram.com/colinismyname

Tumblr
Colinismyname.tumblr.com

Made in the USA
San Bernardino, CA
02 August 2018